WAVE

ANDREW SOFER

MAIN STREET RAG PUBLISHING COMPANY
CHARLOTTE, NORTH CAROLINA

Cover art courtesy of iStockphoto.com
Author photo by: Christopher Soldt

Library of Congress Control Number: 2010933617

ISBN: 978-1-59948-262-0

Produced in the United States of America

Main Street Rag
PO Box 690100
Charlotte, NC 28227
www.MainStreetRag.com

Acknowledgments

My thanks to the editors of the following publications, in which these poems first appeared, sometimes in earlier versions:

Anthology of New England Poets 2006: "Kafka's Farewell"
Atlanta Review: "My Father as a Schoolboy,"
    "Exit Julian, Pursued By a Bear"
Boston College Magazine: "Wittgenstein in Norway,"
    "Advice from Orpheus," "Riddle"
Dogwood: "After the Storm," "Mea She'arim"
Folio: "The Flood" (as "First Romance")
The Formalist: "Cambridgeshire Windmills," "Landing,"
    "The Glenn Gould Variations," "Jerusalem Flowers"
Gargoyle: "Conkers"
Heat City Review: "Kenning"
Iambs & Trochees: "Cambridge Now"
The Lyric: "Cathedral"
Margie: "Walking to Moscow"
North American Review: "Picasso's Saltimbanques"
Poet Lore: "The Anatomy of Whales"
Poetry International: "Ein Kerem"
Poiesis: "Via Dolorosa" (as "Pilgrims")
Southern Poetry Review: "Renting a Tux"
Southwest Review: "Wandlebury Ring," "A Latin Lesson,"
    "Noughts and Crosses"

"Wandlebury Ring," "Noughts and Crosses," and "A Latin Lesson" received *Southwest Review*'s Morton Marr Prize.

"My Father as a Schoolboy" and "Exit Julian, Pursued by a Bear" received *Atlanta Review*'s International Publication Prize.

"Mea She'arim" and "Riddle" received New England Poetry Club's Rosalie Boyle/Norma Farber Award.

"Home, Unpacking" received New England Poetry Club's Erika Mumford Award.

"Cathedral" received *The Lyric*'s Margaret Haley Carpenter Prize.

"Cambridge Now" received First Prize in the *Iambs & Trochees* Contest.

"After the Storm" received New England Poetry Club's Gretchen Warren Award.

"The Anatomy of Whales" was reprinted in *Open Door: A Poet Lore Anthology 1985-1996* (Baltimore: Writer's Center Editions, 1997).

The sheet music to "Wandlebury Ring," set for string quartet and mezzo-soprano by Kevin Beavers, is available from Oxford University Press (2004).

CONTENTS

~

~

WANDLEBURY RING

October, and a mist drifts from the Fens.
I'm eight years old and standing on the downs
of Gog Magog Hill with my family.

It's Sunday, and my brother and I rose early
to pack our lunch and load the stuttering car.
Now we race jagged kites into the air,

wrestling a wind that tugs our fingers numb.
Our father shows us how to make them climb
and twirl like German bombers in the war.

He falls over, plays dead—then swallows air
to chase us screaming round and round the hill.
We make him keep on bombing us until

we flop down and gaze northward toward the Wash.
I imagine stilt-legged fen-folk crossing marsh
two hundred years before, when farms were drowned.

Now skylarks, peewits skirl over lowland.
Gog and Magog, sleeping giants, stretch away.
Below us are the woods of Wandlebury.

We wander into a thick glade of beech
then tread our muddy circle round the ditch
that ancient Britons dug to build their fort.

Father tells how Romans tore it apart,
burning bricks from soft East Anglian clay
to mount their rounded arches toward the sky

and pave the Via Devana to Haverhill.
Down the scarp and into the ditch we tumble,
tramping like soldiers through the fallen leaves

that crunch beneath our feet. The barrow-graves
where Romans piled their dead lie further north,
but here we roll ourselves in rich black earth

then clamber up the bank, smelling of leaf-
mould, wood smoke, dirt, and ash. It's a relief
to shiver and find ourselves on sunlit lawn,

leaving behind the glade and red hawthorn
for the cobbled drive. We cross the slippery bridge
and peer together over its mossy edge

at hungry ducks, the sunken cricket pitch's
forget-me-not. Behind me lies the ditch
where today it is my father's shade I see

kicking dead leaves aside to unbury me.

Andrew Sofer

A LATIN LESSON

They storm in like centurions, my teachers,
pausing to gird their loins or tie their shoes,
then stomping into class as if to war.
Babbage, prefect on watch, shouts a *Cave-ee!*
so we assume our most respectful features,
pretending we can't smell Headmaster's booze,
and jump to stand when Sir comes through the door.
Settle down, boys. Turn to page 33

and Caesar's battles with . . . ahem . . . the Gaul.
Obediently we turn to the dead rows
of words like corpses littered on a stage.
Sofer, you first. Translate where we left off.
My stomach's in perfect tense. *The Roman wall*
's . . . accusative. Or ablative. Who knows?
Might I ask, boy, if you're on the right page?
Sir's nicotined fingers hide a rasping cough.

The Roman . . . ditches? I furtively consult
my *Shorter Latin Primer*, long since inked over
as *Shortbread Eating*. Could it be "the beach"?
What in hell was Caesar doing? Sir opines
Someone else can rescue Gaul, perhaps. Tumult
erupts. *Me, Sir! Me, Sir!* Caesar recovers
as tongue-tied scholars suddenly find speech.
Sofer! Kindly write out one hundred lines:

Tempus fugit. I shan't waste 2A's time.
Sir smirks. His victim's thrown to the lions,
and class drags on till afternoon libations.
One-nil: Rome triumphs, barbarian is humbled.
A hopeless case, I'm sentenced for the crime
of being modern—but Empire declines
once boys learn more exciting conjugations.
Sic biscuitus disintegrat, Sir. Rome crumbled.

Andrew Sofer

THE MASK

They laughed when I begged them to take it down,
a red-faced demon my parents bought in Bali
and couldn't bear to part with. So it hung
on the landing by my room. When I let slip
I knew it hated me, that I hid my eyes
each time I passed the ghastly wooden thing
so it won't see me, my brother guffawed.
For days he'd suddenly become the mask,
prising his mouth wide open with his thumbs
and waggling his tongue at me. *I've got you now!*
I laughed along. Now I could never tell
the secret that still kept me up at night:
how in a dream the glowing mask had whispered
You must believe in evil. And I ran.

HOME FROM SCHOOL

The basement hugs its darkness to itself.
I crouch one floor above its muffled hum.
What did my father hide behind the shelf?

I hold my breath a minute and a half
until at last I hear the front door slam.
The basement hugs its darkness to itself

and I am seven, shrewd as any elf,
as if its jaws might tear me limb from limb.
What did my father hide behind the shelf?

O thief who stole the kingdom, blind yourself.
I lose my footing—stumble—bite my thumb.
Hugging the basement's darkness to myself

I trace the wall that ends in a sheer gulf
of pitch black air. I tighten like a drum.
Whatever Father hid behind the shelf,

he hoards the totem's magic for himself.
I reach into the gloom, my fingers numb.
The basement hugs its darkness to itself.
What did my father hide behind the shelf?

Andrew Sofer

FAMILY RECIPE

Grandmother bows over the dough
dripping salt and grease. She bakes
once every summer *to fatten you up*,
brings gifts from the Holy Land—
a paperweight *shtetl* englobed in snow,
Hanukah *gelt* wrapped in gold—
but scares me when she whispers
This is the way we remember, Skinny,
pinching my wrist. I try not to breathe
in the raw butter as we roll yellowing
letters for the departed—*Blessed be They*—
till our offerings burst from the oven,
the first *A* searing my pursed mouth.

BOOMERANG

I threw the boomerang in such a way
that it would sail beyond our tidy lawn
then double back into my waiting palm.

Instead I watched my new toy slice the air
and catch my mother just above the eye
as if it meant to cut her down to size.

I couldn't make her understand that chance
sometimes takes matter into its own hands,
that aimlessness, as well as rage, can blind.

Andrew Sofer

CAMBRIDGESHIRE WINDMILLS

For Paul

The year we go windmill mad, my brother and I,
we climb up endless rickety stairs that yield
under foot, through rotten hulks that score the sky
and smell of straw and rats. Flat Cambridge fields,
checkerboards of mustard yellow and green,
stretch out toward Norfolk and the river Ouse.
Farmers burn piles of leaves. They dredge up beans,
beets, and—from rich black wormy soil—potatoes.

Here land is an illusion. When fens drown
you have to pump, so black-sailed windmills came
three hundred years ago. I hear them groan
to life as the oak wheels creak then thrum;
not dark satanic mills at all, but djinns
for solemn-faced boys to march round widdershins.

CONKERS

fell from chestnut
trees in prickly burrs, plump
as forbidden fruit. We peeled away
their husk, laying bare the fleshy warriors,
then left them baking in the sun all day.
At Break the boys took turns to let them dangle
from strings of twine, awaiting the first attack.
You'd take your time, nod sagely, gauge the angle,
then flick your wizened conqueror with a *crack!*
that blasted theirs to bits. But by some infernal
luck sometimes the raw seed worked its magic
and we'd bow before the god inside the kernel.
Sing, Muse, an antique tale—epic not tragic:
brash chestnut, brazen even in defeat,
O golden child the world
will roast and
eat.

Andrew Sofer

NOUGHTS AND CROSSES

The day I didn't have to go to school
I watched our silent T.V. screen instead.
The Trade Test Pattern was all I had to fool.
I stared until its frozen colors bled.

I watched our silent T.V. screen instead
of figuring out where Father might have gone.
I stared until its frozen colors bled:
a girl played noughts and crosses with a clown

(figuring out where Father might have gone?)
for hours and hours. I sat there gazing as
a girl played noughts and crosses with a clown.
I didn't see the point, but there I was;

for hours and hours I sat there gazing as
the world contracted to a grinning face.
I didn't see the point, but there I was,
as if by magic I could cross that space,

the world contracted to a grinning face.
Somehow I had to get a message through
as if by magic: I *could* cross that space.
It felt like something that I had to do—

somehow I had to get a message through—
until I cut the X into my skin.
It felt like something that I had to do,
pretending that I couldn't feel a thing.

Until I cut the X into my skin
the Trade Test Pattern was all I had to fool,
pretending that I couldn't feel a thing
the day I didn't have to go to school.

THE FLOOD

As if by accident two fingers clutch,
retreat—rally—curl round their twin again
till clammy palms lock firm. The thing is done
but still a secret, our knees' grazing touch
hidden beneath the table. Drops of rain
spatter the ferry deck and scald my tongue.

A heartbeat floods her cheek, pitching the boat.
Oh! she gulps, then *I think my stocking's run.*
We rise lopsided, hands fused like a chain,
and Mother's chatter catches in her throat.
At sixteen, God, it's begun.

KAFKA'S FAREWELL

Scratching out *The Castle*, plagued
by hemorrhoids, boils, and the TB
uncoiling in his chest like a viper,

how he envied those warm bodies
at Spindelmuhle whizzing past
his window, all schnapps and good cheer.

Did he lie at the bottom of the slope,
black limbs twitching air, target
of catcalls and apple cores?

My situation in this world
would seem to be a dreadful one,
alone here on a forsaken road.

Did he dream of hurtling
down the trail, bowler hat,
stiff collar and scarecrow ears—

then relax into the *schuss*
of it, snowplough to stem christie,
stem christie to parallel turn

as he swoops into the sky
shedding jacket, coat, and hat.
Look, a child cries, *a flying Jew!*

Andrew Sofer

PICASSO'S SALTIMBANQUES

drift from town to town. Fat Grandfather
remembers when inns welcomed tumbling players
who drummed up trade from every alleyway.
He knows that way of life no longer exists,
worries what will become of the little girl.
Who will she marry? How will she live? The sun

glares down unseen. The fat man's frowning son—
scarfed, in motley, young to be a father—
clasps the chalk white wrist of the tiny girl.
She wants to put her arabesque on display where
gentlemen swoon; she'll bow and make her exits,
having long ago thrown her shabby dress away.

Mother's gaze leaves the frame, as if a way
forward presents itself. Her younger son's
gaze bores into her back. Had love existed
between them, we would have to look back further
than the horizon, for each rooted player
seems lost to the others, even the wilting girl

whose roses climb her basket as the girl
thinks back to the clay jug she left halfway
full of water. Her oldest brother sheds layer
after layer, bearing up under midday sun,
yoked to his drum forever. Like his father
he wonders if the next village exists.

Rilke pitied these acrobats who exist
savagely wrung out by will—this girl,
her brothers, father, mother, grandfather—
flung like a heedless child's castaway
toy after convalescence. Still the sun
unfurls them in deserted canvas, players

unraveled by grief's play. They turn away
as if we, too, exist only like the girl,
drawn by our father's hand beneath the sun.

Andrew Sofer

WALKING TO MOSCOW

My older brother sets off for Moscow
wearing thick boots and a thin scarf.

As he leaves London, sleet falls.
He reaches Harwich in a few hours

and walks over the English channel
past astonished ferries. 1990:

he writes that Germany seems full
of people standing in squares

as if listening to important speeches
or deaf. In a Munich campground

a fat man with sad eyes rests
his hand on my brother's knee,

invites him to his tent to drink
Pilsner and listen to Schubert lieder.

My brother refuses. In December
he runs out of food

and begins to consume his past,
starting with his childhood.

My brother never arrives
in Russia. Our grandfather waits

at a crossroads in Kajanadoc
in his old peddler's cart

whose loose wheel will soon
spin off and kill him,

raising his lantern
as it begins to snow.

Andrew Sofer

HOME, UNPACKING

Two woven basket lids from the Old City,
orchid bulb, cinnamon, nutmeg and milk,
Amichai's poems, some crumpled maps,
muezzin's call to the jasmine of rain,
crones of Mahane Yehuda spice market,
my Turkish carpet that never flew,
Ein Gedi leopards elusive as waterfalls,
jazz ricochets off the citadel wall, piss
stench and street strut of Tel Aviv Bus Station,
peach-scented hookahs, mint tea and hashish,
knife flash and shutter slam, beach rats of Jaffa,
tanks that rolled over the feet of my friends,
scabies of Sinai boring tracks in my groin,
foot soles blistered by shooting desert stars.

WESTERN WALL

We bless the bread and wine, our glances
flushed by sabbath candlelight.
Joshua chuckles through his beard,
crumb-strewn, mouth full. *On such a night*

to be in love—that's holy enough.
You blush, pretend you haven't heard.
Hannah's fingers stroke your hair,
conjure her missing daughter's youth.

We cross Gehenna, winding through
Zion Gate, where beside the Wall
Hasidim whirl reeling dances,
bow and chant beneath fringed shawls.

Joshua *davvens*, drunk with prayer.
Carmel's sweetness whets your mouth.

Andrew Sofer

THE SILENT FATHERS

Daughters of Israel! Clothe yourselves modestly!
—sign posted in the ultra-orthodox
neighborhood of Jerusalem

It's not the way the children spat at us,
nor how their glassy eyes narrowed to slits
as they chanted *Whore of Babylon!* at the girl
dressed in slacks, pale arms bared to the sun.

What I recall is how the silent fathers
folded arms to watch the gathering swarm,
waiting to see which blessed son of Israel
would be the first to cast the righteous stone.

EIN KEREM

A lemon tree stands in my yard. Its fruit
by rights is mine. Except the old stone house
I love, which smells of sandalwood and mice,
was Arab—so each dusk the children loot.
Witness the game: when I see them I shout,
when they hear me they run, and in a trice
vanish like sunlight in the olive trees,
leaving their curse behind. It's not about
lemons at all, of course, but who owes what
to whom. Once near this village an angel spoke,
struck mute the doubting priest whose son was born.
Whose language must we speak to pay the debt?
I raise the children's crooked stick and shake
lemon after lemon from silent thorns.

Andrew Sofer

VIA DOLOROSA

Lurching out the Armenian Hospice
into the Christian Quarter's heat,
George's stretcher teems with lice.

Fouad and I cart him up the street,
stumble, stagger, curse our load.
The ladder fell, he broke both wrists.

We rest. A crowd winds down the road,
makeshift crosses clutched in fists.
Leicas whirr, an Ikon glints.

Blocked, the pilgrims halt, stare down
at fractured elbows bound in splints.
Can someone lend a hand? They frown

then shuffle past us, at a loss,
toward the next Station of the Cross.

MEA SHE'ARIM

For my father

Lost in the city late this foggy night,
I stumble past the black-cloaked Hasidim
who dart like shadows through an umber light.
They keep the doorways of Jerusalem,
and I'm a visitor destined to try
one hundred gates, not one of which leads home.
Three thousand miles away, I'm haunted by
your absence, like the coda to a poem
missing some key phrase just out of reach.
A surge of blood, your foot upon the pedal—
that graceful swerve into the local church—
were, in a life of jokes, your final riddle.
Bereft of clues, I stand completely still.
Tell me which door to open, and I will.

Andrew Sofer

JERUSALEM FLOWERS

August inflames stone. Streets scatter
noontime as we crush in buses
eager for crisp sheets, quick love.
Famished ants scour Jaffa Road,
hunched survivors sway and mutter
at girls whose lips beguile like bruises.
Couples sit, too dazed to move.
In parks carnation buds explode.

We speed past pinks in serried rows
whose petals blur this window pane.
I glance up from my paper—things
aren't going well up north again—
and here a soldier stoops to show
sewn on her sleeve, a tank with wings.

HER KEY

Not bothering about you, except not
to lose you or forget what you were for,
I let you tarnish on a copper ring,
rust into unfamiliar peaks and valleys,
give up the spark that raced from lock to palm
each time the tumblers fell like sorcery.

I kept you in my pocket as a charm.
At night you were a magic key, decoding
strangers' voices, cries behind her door.
The blade turned in my mind sharper than thought
of what no longer opened at my touch.
Your living silver, fading by degrees,
caught in my throat like curdled mercury.
I shut you in a drawer to hide how much.

Andrew Sofer

LANDING

I circle through rough cloud, slick yellow moon,
plunge out of black sky this bumpy night
as beach rears up at me, swallowing ocean
beneath the wheels of my half empty flight.
Stretched below lies our last walk to Jaffa
past the sand-buried mosque at evening.
You threw two stones that sank in clotted water,
above our heads a furious jet keened in,
and shadows scuttled over broken glass.
Now nothing stirs on the curved spine below
except a *khamsin* scything tufts of grass.
I swore if I came back you'd never know,
but now I shut my eyes against the view
that spirals past and pulls me in to you.

THE BRIDE

His foot smashes the glass.
My hands tremble,
holding up your *chupa*.

Hennaed ringlets drape
your wedding dress, *Adina*:
she who is gentle.

I came on the night flight,
Tel Aviv palms, Moroccan jazz,
an airport *sherut* with a broken meter.

Two years ago, we said farewell
on the monastery roof,
tongues without translation.

Now I shake your husband's hand.
Your mother tugs him away, cries
for her beloved Baghdad, drunk

in the swirl of the *hora*
we dance together, our last *shalom*
somewhere between goodbye and peace.

Andrew Sofer

OLD CITY

In dreams I walk your streets past every door.
The muezzin calls the blind and lame to prayer.
I have forgotten what I came here for.
I look behind me, but there's no one there.

Damascus Gate. Soldiers are everywhere—
one tips a beggar's cup onto the floor.
My coffee's cold. Some children stop and stare.
In dreams I walk your streets past every door.

Three mangy cats circle outside a store.
I squint against the Quarter's sudden glare.
Is this the place? Have I been here before?
The muezzin calls the lame and blind to prayer.

A shutter clangs. It isn't my affair.
The waiter seems to smile, but I'm not sure.
I pay the bill. The cats aren't anywhere.
I have forgotten what I came here for.

The children follow me beyond the door.
I sweat, pick up the pace. The children stare.
My footsteps echo like a slamming drawer.
I look behind me, but there's no one there.

I turn the corner where a winding stair
leads to a blind alley with no door.
The beggar shuts his eyes and chants a prayer
whose words scatter like coins upon the floor
in dreams I walk.

THE SLAP

Martha's Vineyard, 1969

A wave hits, and I start to sink
as spray arcs in a spangled bow
that glistens as it pulls me in.
I have to fight the urge to drink
blue salt, green sky. *Let go, let go.*

My body spirals, lungs a sheath
of ocean. Plunging from the bank,
my father tugs. I drag below
as if to dare him not to win.
He strikes my cheek. I gasp, choke, breathe.

WITTGENSTEIN IN NORWAY

Skjolden, 1913

I fled my past to wrestle face to face
the demon logic conjured in my brain.
The world was everything packed in my case.
I scorned the Cambridge of the merely sane.

The demon logic conjured in my brain.
I wrote *'A' is the same letter as 'A.'*
Scorning the Cambridge of the merely sane,
what only could be shown I strove to say.

I wrote *'A' is the same letter as 'A.'*
The logic of my trip escaped my friends.
What only could be shown I strove to say,
dirtying a flower with muddy hands.

The logic of my trip: escape my friends
to solve the problems of philosophy—
dirtying a flower with muddy hands,
reducing reason to tautology.

To solve the problems of philosophy
I kicked away the ladder of the mind,
reducing reason to tautology.
The locals wondered what I came to find.

I kicked away the ladder of the mind.
My empty notebooks filled a single shelf.
The locals wondered. What I came to find:
the mirror, language, turned upon itself.

Andrew Sofer

My empty notebooks filled (a single shelf).
The world is everything that is the case.
The mirror language turned upon itself
I fled my past to wrestle face to face.

THE ANATOMY OF WHALES

Hornlike strips inside the upper jaw
crimp into corset stays. Wax ambergris
culled from intestine breeds perfume fixative,
and spermaceti candles, ointments, musk
boil down from fatty acids in the head
whose scrimshawed teeth survive as amulets.

Dolphins, they say, call in dialects,
study in schools, nurse young and mourn lost friends,
while pods of orcas have returned small pets
washed overboard to shore. They hunt in herds
and gather to rouse a mute leviathan,
buoying the body, singing to the drowned.

Tonight I dream of whales plying black ocean:
grief sounding through them like a radio
insistent in its frequency of wave,
joining the kelpies' chorus in the wake
only to let the dead weight fall below,
each note a wreathing spiracle of breath.

Andrew Sofer

CAMBRIDGE NOW

Our living room and dining room are gone,
as is the Garden Room where I would play
the sick piano, bored on my half-terms,
while Mr. Sadler sweated on the lawn.
He'd tip his cap and shift his eyes away,
muttering *Sir*, and I would turn beet red
knowing I was younger than his son.
I helped him pick our apples where they lay
beneath the tree, checking the worst for worms,
their musty bulk rotting the garden shed.

I find the study where my parents worked,
desks side by side, hers in a messy pile
of papers, Freud's complete works, a small fern.
My father's desk was neat. I often lurked
until he left and raided his velvet file
for drawing paper. It put him in a rage.
He'd shout at me until my shoulders jerked
with tears. Then he'd recover, gravely smile
and say he was sorry, but I had to learn
the hidden cost of every wasted page.

My mother's room smelt faintly of cologne
and medicine. Surrounded by her books,
she lay in bed with all the blinds pulled down,
pretending she was talking on the phone.
She used to joke about our firing Cook
but still served Campbell's soup day after day
then crept upstairs to *have a bite* alone.
In later years her *chap* would catch my look

at table, quickly tie his dressing gown,
and help her clear the dirty plates away.

The owner leads me up the creaking stairs.
Perched on a step, I'd read for hours on end,
picking the worn green lino into shreds—
our family never went in for repairs.
My fingers trace the banister round its bend
past the landing to my bedroom door.
I open it expecting stained blue chairs,
the broken spacecraft built for my best friend,
my vampire collection, typewriter, bunk beds.
We put our kitchen on the second floor.

I sit down at a table of stripped pine
and force myself to look. The room is bright
with sun cascading through the window pane
and cheery with a warmth that isn't mine.
It used to get so dark in here at night
I made my mother put a light outside
the door I had to close when I was nine.
My hand shakes, spilling tea. *Are you all right?*
I nod, but at the cracked sink once again
I rinse my eyes, like the day my father died.

Andrew Sofer

CATHEDRAL

Washington, D.C.

I discover the cathedral through bare trees
that only a few weeks ago were full,
but shed a mottled canopy of leaves.

Sitting at your oak desk, I feel the pull
of these new days spent leaning in to you,
testing the weight of silence against words.

A narrow window offers me a view
of quiet air, and a crows' nest where birds
settle between two branches like a Y.

The faint throb of a jet arcs overhead,
and vapor cloud furrows a field of sky
with white that thickens in a hazy spread.

Behind each constellation of ourselves
lie others. I look around our cluttered space
and wonder if by emptying the shelves

of all we've gathered here, we could erase
this sky, these trees, this window, or this love.
The cathedral starts to meld with violet light

seeping through late afternoon mist. Above
stone towers, martins dart and wheel in flight
then blur, lost in a climbing purple stain.

Perhaps a haven is what love requires,
as when ducking in a marble nave past rain
we hear a steeple bell through hollow spires.

Andrew Sofer

ADVICE FROM ORPHEUS

Dull the ear that craves pure tone.
As gravity warps the path of light,
so harmony must bend each one.

Learn to accept, when things fall flat
or sharpness hangs in air, the ruse
we know as *equal temperament*,

that necessary compromise.
No instrument whose pitch is set
can follow if you trade your muse.

Yet sometimes when you stop the fret
a god arrives under the wire,
and for an instant you can get

those overtones you used to hear,
an unexpected telegram
singing the music of the spheres.

THE GLENN GOULD VARIATIONS

Beneath the vaulted windows of a church
the record company sold, he sits once more
at the custom Yamaha. His shoulders hunch
close to the keyboard as he eyes the score
at which, twenty-six years ago, he shone.
Hands dart like startled spiders over keys,
note trills to theme, theme into variation,
only to stop. His ungloved fingers freeze
then cramp. As he ponders arithmetical
architecture, the suture of a phrase—
notes pulsing now like stars inside the skull—
his mind drifts north to chill Toronto days
and Evensong, the priest's lulling refrain,
then through stained glass arpeggios of rain.

Andrew Sofer

AFTER THE STORM

*You taught me language, and my profit on't
Is I know how to curse.*
—Caliban, *The Tempest*

Now they have sailed away and left me here
to share my barren language with the water,
lacking a magic wand or spell to conjure
back the old magician and his daughter,
I spend my days watching the tides go out
or memorizing flight patterns of birds.
Sometimes I move blanched chess pieces about
the rotting board and contemplate the words
king, queen. In Naples, bride of Ferdinand,
how many goodly creatures did you find?

Did salt wind sting your last glimpse of our island
with tears at finally reaching your own kind,
the brave new world you hoped would soon be yours?
Perhaps you pray for me, the snarling wretch
you found a naked savage on all fours,
scrabbling for any beetle he could catch.
You claimed no print of goodness clung to me
and yet I offered everything I knew
when you took hungry refuge from the sea
inside the cave that soon belonged to you.

*I feared you. Even when we played together
you used to tease and, laughing, pull my hair.
My skin was pale, yours dark. I wondered whether
you had been spawned under a wicked star
or if all men were like you except Father:
rough and unkind, smelling of sweat and sea.*

Sometimes I could pretend you were my brother
and pity your not being loved like me.
When we played hide-and-seek each time we fought,
I shuddered as I let myself be caught.

One day I found you weeping on the shore,
grinding your streaming face into the sand.
I ran to look. I'd not seen blood before.
I touched it to my lips; you grabbed my hand
and sucked my finger. So we shared our blood
for the first time. It became our private rite
each time we bled, until the sudden flood
burst from inside. Ashamed, I hid that night
though I could hear you calling out my name.
That was the end of our most secret game.

I fetched and carried while you sat and learned
your father's droning lessons at his table.
You drummed soft fingers slyly as you yawned;
I framed my tongue to every syllable.
You taught me language, yes—so I might curse
my own reflection when I crouched to look
down at a brackish, weed-stricken Narcissus.
We found his picture once in Prospero's book.
You blushed and wondered at his nakedness,
then leapt like flame from my rough tenderness

and told what I had done. I'd only meant
to coil the secret dampness of your hair
around my stubby finger to name its scent—

Andrew Sofer

the streak of salt and waterfall hidden there—
since love was more than a mirror in a pool.
You know I never came that close again,
a breathless Triton reaching for the pearl
offering itself to me. You screamed, and then
your father banished me beneath the rock
where no light shone and where no pictures spoke.

Perhaps I was wrong to pity. I was young.
We came from different blood. When I drank yours,
I'd taste delicious poison on my tongue.
I drink rich wines now. Ferdinand ignores
the trace of bitterness left in my mouth
and seeks out sweeter pleasures in the port.
I could not bear the blowflies of the south
so traveled north to my poor father's court.
He has grown old and tired. We sit and pray
in silence for the thing we dare not say.

Winter creeps by me now upon cold sand.
My sounds and sweet airs vanished in a wind
that howled to hear the cracking of his wand
as he turned his back, leaving dead wood behind.
My every third thought shall be my grave
were his last words. You wondered what he meant—
the closest thing to love he ever gave.
I think on him, his dark acknowledgment,
and picture an old man after the storm
trailing a thin dry stick under his arm.

KNIFE TO THUMB

For my mother

Sam's taken to pruning naked on the lawn,
muttering obscenities to himself,
shooting at squirrels with his BB gun.

She's sixty-five, he's eighty. Every year
this house sucks up more trouble than it's worth.
Another mouse found floating in the drain,
a yard of weeds she can't get help to clear.

He says she never listens and won't cook
a decent meal these days. He can't forgive her
making him sell his one-room cabin, where
he taught sons carpentry. *I'm like a guest*

he whines, and keeps on getting in the way.
She slices lemons in the sunlit kitchen,
knife to thumb, just as her mother taught.
Keep moisture in, let all the sourness out.

At night they watch his favorite nature shows,
drinking cocktails by the flickering light
as creeper winds its way around the porch
and insects slam themselves against the glass.

Andrew Sofer

KENNING

1. Renting a Tux

Off the cuff, I wonder how many men,
bit players grooming for the major part,
have squeezed their frames to fit the shape I'm in.

Buttonholed by bores year after year,
we parcel out our lives in cummerbunds.
Surely it pays to purchase what we rent?

And yet how comforting to follow suit,
to wear our hearts on someone else's sleeve
and, made to measure, dance in borrowed time.

2. A Brooklyn Wedding
Prospect Park, 1995

Despite the glow of our romance
we don't attract a second glance,
a just-wed couple dressed in white
out for a stroll this warm June night.

Filling a corner of a canvas
out of Breughel's *Icarus*,
we make our splash and drift away,
flotsam of this Saturday.

Andrew Sofer

3. Wanting a Child

A Vineyard summer
of storms, our garden ablaze
with whorled irises.

At night we rub ice
on each other's beaded skin,
doze, wrestle drenched sheets.

Jellyfish thicken
the lagoon. An osprey flits,
shadowed by cygnets.

We wake to gnashing
screeches outside our window
shrill as a banshee.

Under gravid moon
I crane a bristled neck, glimpse
eyes ringed like targets.

4. At the Fertility Clinic

The idea was to give a fighting chance:
invite athletic dancers to the dance
but leave each wilted wallflower behind.

It wasn't the ordeal I came to mind.
I grew to dread the sympathetic smile
the nurse gave me with every wasted vial.

Andrew Sofer

5. Riddle

Show me your face before you were born.
What left its trace? Before you were born

singularity blossomed. Its needle's point
wove time into space before you were born.

A mirror hung in the balance and shattered.
We threw salt just in case, before you were born.

You lodged in the reeds. Pharaoh's daughter
knelt in embrace before you, weir-borne.

Heartbeat's saccade, hoof's capriole
galloped apace before you were born.

Sometimes there's God — so quickly, said Blanche.
Ineffable grace: before you, we're born.

Child, in sleep you climb ladders of air
dreams held in place before you were born.

I, a scribe, write in my father's Cyrillic.
His was my face before you were born.

6. Exit Julian, Pursued By a Bear

He's scared that bears will eat him once I leave,
so every night I build a Plato's cave
of sofa cushions, then hide his teddy there—
convenient stand-in for Idea of Bear—

for Julian to hunt to his heart's content.
Though we pretend the game is innocent,
we know the beast that hungers for my boy
bears scant resemblance to his cuddly toy.

Some days you eat the bear, the Russians say,
some days the bear eats you. At end of play
he'll enter darkness, knowing I can't share it.
Already he has learned to grin and bear it.

Andrew Sofer

7. Kenning

Stamping his bare feet at breakers' edge,
Julian shrieks and spreads his fingers wide
our last day at the ocean. I'm nearby
half reading *Beowulf*, half watching him
yell *Waves, go back to England! Go away!*

I want to tell my Canute of the New World
how *stalwart warriors once sailed oar-steeds*
athwart the whale-road, under a world-candle.
But he's too young for kenning. So I rise
and take his hand, entering deeper water

neither of us can name, although we taste
its music — salt cacophony of wave
crashing its cymbals for an empty sky —
while at our back the sea resolves itself
by drowning out those words we've left behind.

MY FATHER AS A SCHOOLBOY

Lions at the nearby zoo roar me to sleep.
They echo the roars we once heard at Tsavo,
where at dusk elephants came to lick salt
from the pools by our cabin, dung beetles
crunched under my feet like cobblestones.

In my dream, I climb Table Mountain.
Under dazzling sun, I reach the plateau.
Far below, a schoolboy on a class outing,
you carve your name in rock, dream
of diving into the cool bay. Tonight

you will copy your oldest brother's essay
in Afrikaans: *My Day on The Mountain.*
You will be the fifth brother to hand it in.
It will not be your children's language.
You are the last brother on the mountain.

I want to reach down to you, restless boy
who will seek your fortune in a rainy land,
tell you to seize the Cape of Good Hope,
an ocean glimpsed through a cloth of cloud
that spills into air like a breaking wave.

Andrew Sofer

Notes

"A Latin Lesson." "Cave-ee," from the Latin *cave* ("beware"), is an English schoolboy cry that signals a schoolmaster's approach. Writing one hundred identical lines is a traditional punishment for a minor infraction. *Tempus fugit*: Time flies. *Sic biscuitus disintegrat*: That's the way the cookie crumbles.

"Conkers." A sonnegram (sonnet-calligram) for John Hollander. The chestnut appears in Homer, Pindar, Virgil, Pliny, Martial, Galen, and other ancient writers.

"Noughts and Crosses." The English name for tic-tac-toe. The Trade Test Pattern, as described in the poem, used to be broadcast on British television whenever regular programming ceased.

"The Flood." The curtal sonnet was invented by Gerard Manley Hopkins.

"Kafka's Farewell." The italicized passage was written by Franz Kafka in Spindelmuhle, a Silesian ski resort, in 1922. He died two years later.

"Picasso's Saltimbanques." Picasso's 1905 painting *Family of Saltimbanques*, which inspired Rilke's Fifth Duino Elegy, hangs in the National Gallery of Art in Washington, D.C.

"Western Wall." Mount Carmel was traditionally known as the "vineyards of God." Carmel is a popular brand of kosher wine. *Davven* is a Yiddish word for pray.

"Ein Kerem" ("Well of the Vineyard") is a village on the western edge of Jerusalem. According to tradition, Mary and her cousin Elizabeth, John the Baptist's mother, met joyously in Ein Kerem while both were pregnant. Both pregnancies were foretold by the angel Gabriel, who struck dumb Elizabeth's husband Zachariah in the temple when he doubted the prophecy (Luke 1:8-39).

"Mea She'arim," literally one hundred gates or doors, is the ultra-orthodox neighborhood of Jerusalem.

"Landing." The *khamsin* is a hot desert wind that blows across Egypt and Israel.

"Wittgenstein in Norway." The italicized quotations are taken from Ludwig Wittgenstein's letters and journals, 1913-14.

"Cambridge Now." The rhyme scheme is borrowed from Philip Larkin's poem "Faith Healing."

"Advice from Orpheus." Equal temperament, the European system which divides the octave into twelve evenly spaced notes, standardized natural acoustics in the mid-seventeenth century.

"After the Storm." The first speaker is Caliban, the second (in italics) Miranda. The italicized quotation in the last stanza is from *The Tempest*'s final scene.

"Riddle." "Show me your face before you were born" is a famous ko'an (Zen riddle). Blanche's line is from *A Streetcar Named Desire*. In Hebrew, a *sofer* is a scribe or author.

"Exit Julian, Pursued By a Bear." The stage direction "*Exit, pursued by a bear*" is from *The Winter's Tale*.

"Kenning." A type of compound metaphor common in Old Norse and Old English poetry. It can also refer to the limit of vision at sea.

"My Father as a Schoolboy." Tsavo is a game reserve in Kenya. Table Mountain overlooks Cape Town, South Africa.

Special Thanks

I am indebted to many people, among them William Baer, Kevin Beavers, Ben Birnbaum, William Bolcom, Kim Bridgford, Robert Chibka, Geraldine Connolly, Mary Crane, Brian Culhane, my publisher M. Scott Douglass, Kim Garcia, Dana Gioia, Elizabeth Graver, Linda Gregerson, Atar Hadari, Rachel Hadas, the late Sarah Hannah, Kate Henchman, Daniel Hoffman, John Hollander, Stephanie Houtzeel, Andrew Hudgins, Judith Issroff, Marjorie Janis, Ilya Kaminsky, Daphne Leighton, Jeffrey Levine, Steve and Ellen Levine, Kate Light, Paul Mariani, David Mason, Suzanne Matson, the late Frederick Morgan, Richard Peabody, Charlotte Reiter, Martha Rhodes, Jona Rosenfeld, David Sanders, Maxim Shrayer, Elaine Sofer, Michael Sowder, Willard Spiegelman, A. E. Stallings, Henry Taylor, Richard Tillinghast, Daniel Tobin, Andrew Von Hendy, Kevin Walzer, Rosanna Warren, Leah Weed, Russell Whitehead, the late Ruth Whitman, and Greg Williamson.

I am grateful to my writing groups in Washington, D.C. and Ann Arbor; the Writer's Center, Bethesda; Wanda Fleck and the Brooklyn Friends of Chamber Music; Wyatt Prunty and the Sewanee Writers' Conference; Michael Peich and the West Chester University Poetry Conference; Joan Houlihan and the Colrain Manuscript Conference; Rhina Espaillat and the Powow River Poets; and my English department colleagues and deans at Boston College.

Loving thanks to my wife, Bonnie Tenneriello, and son, Julian Sofer.

This book was completed with financial assistance from Boston College and the National Endowment for the Arts.

The author photograph is by Christopher Soldt.